Also by Richard Paul Evans

The Walk Series
The Walk
Miles to Go
The Road to Grace
A Step of Faith

A Winter Dream
Lost December
Promise Me
The Christmas List
Grace
The Gift
Finding Noel
The Sunflower
A Perfect Day
The Last Promise

The
FOUR DOORS

A GUIDE TO
JOY, FREEDOM, AND A
MEANINGFUL LIFE

Richard Paul Evans

SIMON & SCHUSTER

New York   London   Toronto   Sydney   New Delhi

Simon & Schuster
1230 Avenue of the Americas
New York, NY 10020

First Simon & Schuster hardcover edition October 2013

SIMON & SCHUSTER and colophon are registered trademarks
of Simon & Schuster, Inc.

For information about special discounts for bulk purchases,
please contact Simon & Schuster Special Sales at
1-866-506-1949 or business@simonandschuster.com.

The Simon & Schuster Speakers Bureau can bring authors
to your live event. For more information or to book an event,
contact the Simon & Schuster Speakers Bureau at
1-866-248-3049 or visit our website at www.simonspeakers.com.

Interior design by Akasha Archer

Manufactured in the United States of America

10 9 8 7 6 5 4 3 2 1

Library of Congress Control Number: 2013948921

ISBN 978-1-4767-2817-9
ISBN 978-1-4767-2818-6(ebook)

ACKNOWLEDGMENTS

I am grateful for my wife and to have been blessed with such a companion on my earthly sojourn. I am grateful for my parents, both of whom have passed on: my mother who, in her good times, taught me tenderness and love, and my father who taught me to work and to question. I wish to acknowledge my publisher, Jonathan Karp, who from the first time he heard about this book wanted to publish it and had the courage and faith in me to do so. And my agent and dear friend, Laurie Liss, for her enthusiasm for *The Four Doors.*

The Four Doors has been a thirty-year journey for me and throughout this process my thoughts, mind, and heart have been shaped by many books and essays written by brilliant, inspired authors. Their teachings have shaped not only my life but every book I've written. These authors include: Og Mandino, C. S. Lewis, M. Scott Peck, Marianne Williamson, Dr. George G. Ritchie, Dr. Wayne Dyer, and Don Miguel Ruiz.

I am grateful for all those who have asked that I put these principles down on paper. This book is for you and those you love.

For my Heavenly Father,
for His guidance, love and blessings,
including those that came in disguise.

The most important story we will ever
write in life is our own—
not with ink, but with our choices.
—From my book *The Gift*

THE FOUR DOORS

Why I Wrote This Book

A little more than a decade ago, I was signing books in Dayton, Ohio, when one of my readers, a schoolteacher, handed me an envelope filled with money. "My students raised this for your charity for abused children," she said. Then she asked, "Is there any way you could come thank them?"

I was in Dayton for another day, so I set a time to meet her students the following afternoon. I had expected to visit with the students, thank them for their contribution, and say a few words on the importance of reading and literacy. When I arrived at the venue, I was surprised to find buses waiting outside. Unbeknownst to me, my visit to a few students had been turned into a district-wide assembly. "You have an hour to talk to the youth," the teacher said to me.

As I frantically considered what I would say to this room full of students, the idea came to me to share with them everything I wished I knew when I was their age.

That's precisely what I did. For the next hour I spoke from the heart, and the teens sat in complete silence. About halfway through my talk, I noticed that some of the youth were crying. When I finished, the students stood to applaud, then lined up to meet me. Some of them wanted to share with me their own stories and struggles. Some of them just asked to be hugged.

That afternoon was the beginning of a journey

for me, one that has taken me all around the world, sharing this message with hundreds of thousands of people from remarkably diverse groups ranging from the American Mothers, Inc., Harvard MBA graduates, and the Million Dollar Round Table (a global association of the world's top insurance agents and financial service professionals) to recovering drug addicts and convicted felons. And just like the first time I shared these principles, in each of those subsequent presentations I have also witnessed a powerful reaction. And, after every presentation, audience members have asked for a written copy of my talk so that they too could share these principles with those they care about. This book is the result of those requests.

Initially, my talk didn't have a name and I just referred to it as "the talk." It was more than five years after that first presentation before I began calling my talk "The Four Doors." I liked the metaphor of the door for two reasons. First, because passing through a door requires knowledge, intent, and action. We can't pass through a door we can't find and we can't pass through a door without moving ourselves.

Second, once we've crossed a door's threshold, we are not in the same place as we were before. These characteristics are true for each of the doors, or principles, in this book.

I believe that the greatest thing that all humanity has in common is the desire to make their lives matter. In the last two decades, I have met thousands of people and heard many of their stories. Far too many are living what Thoreau termed "lives of quiet desperation." They live far below their own potential for joy, accomplishment, and power, caged in the prisons of their own unknowing. To some degree, this describes all of us.

The Four Doors is about how to live life joyfully, with freedom, power, and purpose. I have witnessed the powerful effect each of these doors carries—in both my own life and the lives of those with whom I have shared this message. If you are willing to follow even just one of these principles, you will find immediate, positive change in your life. If you choose to live them all, you will soon be in a very different place than you are now. The choice is yours. And, as you will soon learn, the Four Doors are entirely about choice.

Foundations

Throughout my writing career, I've discovered, with some amusement, that bookstores aren't always sure how to classify my novels. I've found my books shelved in the literature, romance, philosophy, popular authors, inspirational, spiritual, self-help, and religion sections of bookstores.

If you asked *me* what I think I write, I'd tell you that I pen stories that explore the human experience and impart inspirational ideas about life. This book is a compilation of my beliefs presented in a nonfiction format.

By way of full disclosure, I believe in God. I'm pretty much out of the closet about that. More specifically, I believe in an all-loving, purposeful God who is willing to give us hard things so we might spiritually progress: not a made-for-Sunday-night-movie Deity whose only goal is, at the end of the day, to make sure a good time was had by all. That kind of being would be as impotent and uncaring as a parent whose only goal in sending their child off to college was to give them a place to party. Life is difficult. But it is also purposeful. And, spoiler alert, in the end, love wins.

In addition to this overriding premise, there are three foundational truths upon which the Four Doors rest. Without these truths there would be no reason for this book, as personal change would be pointless and impossible. In addition to my belief in God, these principles comprise the core of my personal belief system and I believe are, to a large degree, self-evident.

SELF-WILL

First, the greatest power and gift humanity possesses, and will ever possess, is the freedom of self-will. All our successes and accomplishments come from the personal exercise of our wills. So do our greatest failures and mistakes. In even the most coercive of circumstances, we have the option of exercising our wills. As Dr. Viktor E. Frankl, a renowned psychiatrist and Holocaust survivor, wrote in his seminal book *Man's Search for Meaning,*

> *Everything can be taken from a man but one thing: the last of human freedoms—to choose one's attitude*

in any given set of circumstances, to choose one's own way.

While it is possible to relinquish our freedom, in degrees and in totality, even the act of giving up our power of choice is, in itself, a choice.

SPIRITUAL EVOLUTION

Second, we are not an accident of God or nature. The universe is demonstrably purposeful, and there's a purpose for our being here on this earth. The experiences we have have come to us for our spiritual growth and evolution. Simply stated, earth is a school—a divine educational process custom-fit to each of us.

THE POSSIBILITY OF CHANGE

We are all in motion. Always. Those who are not climbing toward something are descending toward nothing.

—From my book *Miles to Go*

Third, personal change is not only possible—it is inevitable. The only constant in nature is change, and everything—from galaxies to atoms—is in a continual state of flux. That includes us. Our bodies age, our muscles grow or atrophy, we gain and lose as many as a million cells a day.

Our spiritual being is no more static than our physical one. And, like our physical state, change in our spiritual being also comes from the exercise of will. Whereas certain physical choices, such as whether to eat well or to exercise, will have both short- and long-term consequences on our physical bodies, our spiritual choices also affect our spiritual well-being and growth. We grow or diminish spiritually as we move closer to light or darkness, love or hate, forgiveness or resentment, peace or anguish.

The fact that we are changing is a given. *How* we change is in direct correlation to our choices and the power and exercise of our free will.

The Nature of Change

Every revolution was first a thought
in one man's mind.
—RALPH WALDO EMERSON

All creation begins in the mind as a thought or idea. Though all thoughts do not originate within our minds, that which we choose to focus on grows in significance. The power to focus and direct our thoughts is, in itself, an act of will. In order to change our circumstances physically, we begin by changing them mentally, focusing our thoughts on a specific idea, thereby nurturing the idea. The ultimate potential of an idea may be far more than we can comprehend.

The Power of an Idea

On July 16, 1945, at an army testing site in the desert near Alamogordo, New Mexico, the first atomic bomb was tested. No one who had gathered that day to witness the blast was sure what would happen. In fact, there was a pool among scientists about how big the explosion would be. There was an outside chance, voiced one scientist, that the bomb would set off a nuclear chain reaction that would destroy the entire universe.

While the universe was spared, the explosion was enormous, its energy equivalent to that released by *40 million pounds of dynamite*—equal to all the energy produced and consumed in the United

States every thirty seconds: that's every car, lamp, dishwasher, airplane, diesel train, factory, everything. However, this energy was released in a few millionths of a second, and in a volume only a few inches wide.

The resulting explosion was terrible. The hundred-foot steel tower on which the bomb was mounted was completely vaporized. The cloud formed by the explosion boiled up to a height of thirty-five thousand feet, higher than Mount Everest. For hundreds of yards around the blast site, the surface of the desert sand turned to glass.

Remarkably, the atom that started the explosion was so small that a million of them, lined end to end, would roughly be the width of a human hair.

The atom is the perfect metaphor of an idea. Like the atom, the infinitesimally small spark of an idea can start a chain reaction that will not only change our lives, but possibly even the world. The Egyptian pyramids, democracy, communism, the

Great Wall of China, even the atomic bomb—each began as an idea in *one* mind. These ideas, once shared, interacted with others' ideas, which set off a chain reaction that grew in force until they were of sufficient energy to create massive physical change.

Just as important as the physical manifestations that new ideas can spark are the permanent internal changes that take place within our own minds. Oliver Wendell Holmes wrote,

Man's mind, once stretched by a new idea, never regains its original dimensions.

To understand the truth of this assertion, just consider the global impact of ideas such as Christianity, communism, or evolution.

Magnets and Maps

A new idea, once accepted in our minds, becomes a *mental magnet:* a collecting point for similar and complementary ideas. These ideas collect as mental pictures, stories, legends, philosophies, ideas, etc. Psychologists sometimes refer to this compilation of beliefs as our *mental maps.* We all have mental maps. Many fail to recognize that these maps are no more the real world than a folded paper road map is a paved road. These maps are merely symbolic representations designed to help us reach destinations—literally and figuratively. Unfortunately, mental maps *always* contain errors.

Our maps, initially drawn during infancy and childhood, are powerful and difficult to change. There's a good reason for this. These maps were created for our survival. This is why years after they have become outdated, even obsolete, we still persist in clinging to them—transferring outdated interpretations of past experiences to new and unrelated conditions. This is like concluding that since a road map of Chicago had guided you through that city, it would serve you just as well in Beijing.

Unfortunately, the erroneous zones of our mental maps are usually not as easy to spot as those on paper. It takes discovery, work, and focus to correct them. Some people never go to the trouble. To these people, life seems confusing and stacked against them, just like it would to someone trying to navigate downtown Beijing from a map of Chicago.

Any alteration to our mental map can have a very real effect on how we see the world. But change doesn't come easily, and most people spend more time defending their beliefs than seeking truth. There are two main reasons we resist changing our maps.

First, to significantly alter or abandon a belief system is to leave us vulnerable in a dangerous world—an understandably terrifying proposition.

Second, we've learned that most of the ideas that come to us *should be filtered.* There was a time when people believed just about everything they heard on the radio or television or read in the newspaper. Media advertisements were considered gospel. So was Walter Cronkite. So was the Gospel, for that matter. But we soon learned that sometimes the "truth" wasn't truth. We discovered, oftentimes painfully, that the "truth" being fed to us was sometimes skewed by commercial motives, ulterior agendas, or others' flawed maps. Eventually, experience taught us to filter out most of what we hear. We learned discernment.

Discernment is a blessing. If we didn't screen out the incredible amount of information that bombards us daily, we would be changing in impractical and ridiculous ways.

Still, our maps do change. They change as we progress through formal education. They change because of new experiences and from meeting new people. They change because of the books we read.

Some changes come through repeated media propaganda: commercial, social, and political messages, all of which have ulterior motives.

Significant change comes to our maps when significant things happen to us, like trauma, loss, and illness. For instance, research shows that people are more likely to make a major life change after someone close to them has died.

On some level, all honest and mentally healthy adults accept that their mental maps—if they are even aware of them—contain incongruities and falsehoods. They have discovered through life's experiences that sometimes their maps fail them or lead them to unintended destinations. This is why so much money is spent on counseling, self-improvement courses, and self-help books. Wise people want accurate maps. And accurate maps require a devotion to honesty, study, and experimentation.

This might seem like a lot of work. But life *is a lot of work*. Operating with a faulty mental map only makes it more difficult. On the other hand, few things promise more excitement and joy than learning, self-discovery, and self-improvement.

The purpose of *The Four Doors* is to help you correct and alter your mental map in ways that bring lasting and positive change.

As you honestly examine and challenge your

existing mental map, you may feel that your eyes have been opened to a new world. It's not that the world has changed, rather your view of it has. This is an exciting proposition—one filled with tremendous excitement, possibility, and potential for change. I wish you well on your journey of self-discovery and growth.

Believe There's a Reason You Were Born

Believe There's a Reason You Were Born

Believe. Believe in your destiny and the star from which it shines. Believe you have been sent from God as an arrow shot from His own bow.

It is the single universal trait that the great of this earth have all shared, while the shadows are fraught with ghosts who roam the winds with mournful wails of regret on their lips.

Believe as if your life depended on it . . . for indeed it does.

—From my book *The Locket*

It may sound odd to hear this from a novelist, but my favorite books have always been biographies. In the last decade I've read about the lives of more than two hundred individuals who have changed the world—a list comprising a broad spectrum of overachievers, from Archimedes to Charlemagne and Adolf Hitler to Steve Jobs.

In studying the lives of these individuals I soon found myself asking this question:

Why are some people able to accomplish so much with their lives—sufficient to change the course of history—while most of humanity passes through life barely making a ripple in their own small ponds?

It's a profound question, really. What is it that makes the world changers different than the rest of us? Is there an identifiable personality trait or mindset?

I was reading a book on George Washington

when the answer to that question struck me. As widely as the personalities and accomplishments of those I had studied ranged, I realized that there was a common denominator, one trait that was nearly universal among all of them. It was this:

Almost without exception, history's great achievers held a highly developed sense of personal mission. Nearly every one of them believed that their life had a purpose—that they had something of importance to share with the world.

For some of these individuals, parents or mentors had instilled this sense of purpose. Others just seemed to come by it naturally, as if they had been born with it, or it had flowed into them from some supernal source. Whatever the origin of this belief, each of these greats, in his or her own way, demonstrated this mindset as the impetus behind their momentous lives. Counter to the modern belief of an "accidental existence," the belief that we were born for a reason has the power to radically alter our mental maps. Indeed, it may become our very compass.

MY PERSONAL BELIEF
IN A DIVINE LIFE MISSION

The power of believing in a personal mission is a principle that has had an impact on my own life and has led me to achieve things that I would have never dreamed possible.

When I was twelve years old, my grandfather, a very spiritual man, gave me a blessing in which I was told that I would someday "walk with the royalty of this earth."

I held to his words through the difficulties of my childhood and teenage years. Still, by my late twenties, my grandfather's blessing seemed just as far away as it had to me as a boy. A business I had started was failing, my health was poor, and my marriage was struggling. How would I ever "walk with royalty"? One evening, I went back to my grandfather to see if he had another blessing. He thought about it for a moment and then said, "Yes, I do."

He again placed his hands on my head and began to repeat, almost verbatim, the same blessing he had pronounced almost twenty years previous—with one exception. He added a line. "My beloved grandson," he said, "you are about to embark upon a mission that will touch the hearts of the children of men in a way you now cannot fathom."

I went away confused. *How could this be?* I wondered. Yet something in my heart believed his words. A few months later, I began writing a little Christmas story called *The Christmas Box,* a book that spread throughout the world with more than eight million copies in print worldwide.

Five years later, I was invited to lunch at the home of former President George Bush and Barbara Bush in Houston, Texas. With us that day were their son, President George W. Bush, and British Prime Minister John Major.

That evening, as I took the podium to speak at Mrs. Bush's literacy conference, I glanced down to the front row of that auditorium where sat the First Lady, two U.S. presidents, and a British prime minister. Then I looked out over the audience of thousands and said, "Mrs. Bush, I would be remiss to let this moment pass. When I was twelve years old I was told that someday I would walk with the royalty of this earth. Tonight you see the fulfillment of a promise to a small boy."

Shakespeare wrote, "There's a divinity that shapes our ends." My personal belief in a divine life mission has brought me hope, understanding, and meaning throughout my life.

WHAT IS *MY* LIFE'S MISSION?

There are specific moments in each life
given us to influence our life paths—a
cosmic pull of a lever that switches the
tracks beneath us. History abounds in
such "accidents." If such providence is
evident in the lives of the great,
then why not the rest of us?
—From my book *The Christmas Box Miracle*

One of the questions I'm most frequently asked is, "How do I find my life mission?" An inspired answer to that question was given by Bishop T. D. Jakes:

If you can't figure out your purpose, figure out your passion. For your passion will lead you right into your purpose.

This has been true for me. However, as a believer in Divine intervention, I also believe that we are sometimes given specific direction to fulfill our missions. This Divine guidance comes to us in the form of personal inspiration and experiences. Oftentimes these experiences are painful and, by nature, must be, to give us the power we need to take extraordinary action.

These life-altering experiences also include meeting new people. Life is not a solitary affair and was never meant to be. On our individual journeys, there are companions placed along the trail, fellow sojourners who forever alter our paths and help determine our destination.

PROMPTINGS AND THE INNER VOICE

Implicit in our belief in a divine life mission is the importance of listening to those internal voices that may direct us for good.

Gandhi spoke freely of the need to follow the *still small voice* within us. Ralph Waldo Emerson wrote, "None of us will ever accomplish anything excellent or commanding except when he listens to this whisper which is heard by him alone."

I have heard that whisper on many occasions. Before my first book became a bestseller, I traveled across the country promoting my book. One night in San Diego, California, I was driving away from a disappointing book signing when I had a powerful impression that I should pull off the road into a parking lot. I didn't know why, but I had learned to follow that inner voice.

I had no sooner pulled my car into a parking space and shut off the engine when there was a knock on my back window. I opened the door to see a woman with her two small children.

"Sir, my children are hungry," she said. "Can you feed them?"

That night I had dinner with Angel, Mary, and Bobby at a Jack-in-the-Box restaurant.

The voice of intuition or inspiration has guided my life in ways that astound me. But I know I'm not alone in such experiences. I've heard many similar stories echoed by others. You likely have your own.

ASK

Ask, and it shall be given you;
seek, and ye shall find;
knock, and it shall be opened unto you.
—Matthew 7:7

I believe that in order to fulfill our life mission it is vital that we ask for Divine assistance in our lives. There is tremendous power in desire, and the unseen powers of divinity that affect our lives are oftentimes just waiting for us to ask for their aid. I believe these forces must wait for our request because they are bound by the law of free will and cannot intervene in our lives until we exercise our will and request their assistance.

SUMMARY

"The mystery of human existence
lies not in just staying alive,
but in finding something to live for."
— Fyodor Dostoyevsky

The first step in finding our life purpose is to *believe* in a life purpose. Never underestimate the power of belief. As a tool for shaping our maps, belief is as powerful as knowledge and sometimes more so. History confirms this. Many of the greatest causes initiated by humankind were motivated by faith.

There is one other reason the First Door is so important. To accept that there is a reason we were born is to begin to understand who we really are: We are not a mistake of God or nature.

DOOR TWO

Free Yourself from Limitation

Free Yourself from Limitation

I t may seem overly simplistic to say it, but to achieve our life mission we must *be free* to achieve it.

The definition of freedom is a slippery thing. Too often we speak of freedom as an absolute rather than in terms of measured degrees of personal liberty. For instance, we claim to have freedom of speech, but that does not grant us the freedom to say whatever we want without reproach or punishment. This is a good thing. Absolute freedom for one would result in limited freedom for another.

What we should hope for, and to a large extent currently enjoy, is freedom as an ability to pursue happiness within reasonable and ethical bounds. As such, the greatest impediment to most of our personal freedom is not created by government regulation, but resides within our own heads. It is my experience that the most insidious of limitations are psychological in nature. Three of the most common of these psychological cages are paradigm, victimhood, and fear.

THE CAGE OF PARADIGM

Don't be content with things as they are.
The earth is yours
and the fullness thereof.
—Winston Churchill

The cage of paradigm is an especially effective prison because most people fail to even recognize its existence and its effect on their lives and choices. The definition of a paradigm is:

An intellectual perception or view, accepted by an individual or a society as a clear example, model, or pattern of how things work in the world.

In scientific discovery, when paradigm becomes an obstacle to progress, it is referred to as paradigm paralysis: *the inability or refusal to see beyond the current models of thinking.*

The cage of paradigm refers to those expectations and limits that we, and those around us, use to define ourselves, our abilities, and our potential. These shackles of paradigm are stronger than you probably realize.

External Paradigm

A popular term among Filipinos is *"crab mentality."* The phrase refers to the dynamic of a pot of crabs. Individually, the crabs could easily climb out of the pot, except that the other crabs will pull down any crab that tries to escape.

The analogy to the human condition is obvious. It is a common social phenomenon that members of a group will attempt to "pull down" any individual member who achieves success beyond the others. The mindset is "If I can't have it, neither can you." It is arguable that America is becoming a giant crab pot.

Instead of being inspired by others' success, small-minded people (and this represents a significant percentage of the population) resent others' achievements because they fear that they are being left behind.

I recently came across the story of a formerly obese woman who had, remarkably, lost more than three hundred pounds. She reported that the most difficult challenge to her lifestyle change was that her husband, who was also morbidly obese, worked to sabotage her effort to lose weight. Nearly every day he brought her chocolate and donuts, then acted hurt when she resisted his "gifts." When she accused him of attempting to wreck her diet, he staunchly denied it.

Only after she had lost the weight did her husband admit that he was afraid that once she was thin she would leave him.

> The worst part of success is trying to find
> someone who is happy for you.
> — BETTE MIDLER

My wife and I experienced the effects of crab mentality firsthand. With the success of my first book, *The Christmas Box,* our world changed in some negative ways that we did not expect. Friends stopped talking to us, family stopped visiting, false rumors were spread through our neighborhood about us. It was a difficult time, one that required a lot of forgiving.

When I told my father about what was happening to us, he wisely replied, "You have to understand that your success will always remind others of their failures."

Internal Paradigm

As difficult as it is to transcend others' paradigms, usually the most difficult "crab in the pot" is ourselves. It is our own negative belief and self-talk that keeps us down. "I'm just that way. I can't help it. I've always been poor. I'm not good at that. I have bad luck." These phrases, born of flawed mental maps, run through our minds, fighting our efforts to change.

The Buffet

A few years ago, I wrote this parable to help illustrate how the cage of paradigm operates:

A man was hungry and looking for a place to eat when he spotted a sign outside a restaurant that read:

ALL YOU CAN EAT BUFFET, JUST ONE DOLLAR

He walked inside the restaurant where he found another sign that read:

PLEASE SEAT YOURSELF

The man walked to a small table in a crowded corner of the restaurant. A waitress soon greeted him. "What can I get for you, sir?"

"I'll have the one-dollar special."

"The special?" she asked.

He motioned to the people around him. "Yes, I'll have what they're having."

She handed him a plate. "Help yourself."

There was a long line at the buffet table, and when he finally reached the food, he was unimpressed with what he found. The selection was meager, the food mediocre, and most of the bins were empty or appeared to have been well picked over. *No wonder it's only a dollar,* he thought. He took what he thought he could stomach, then went back to his table disenchanted and grumbling about the fare.

After he finished his meal, he walked to the checkout counter, where the same waitress who had served him stood next to the cash register. Only as he pulled out his wallet did he notice a doorway leading to another room in the restaurant.

This other room was larger and much less crowded than where he had dined. Even though there were fewer people inside, there were long tables laden with food, including many of his favorite dishes: shellfish and thick steaks, breads of all varieties, colorful, plump vegetables, and large platters of cakes, chocolate truffles, and desserts of all kinds. A chef stood at one end of the room slicing great slabs of roast beef.

The man asked the waitress, "How much is that buffet?"

"One dollar," she replied.

"It costs the same as the buffet out here?"

She nodded. "Everything in the restaurant is the same price."

"Why didn't you tell me about that room?"

She looked at him with a perplexed expression. "You said you wanted what everyone else was having."

This is precisely how most people live their lives. It's why they wear what they wear, drive what they drive, live where they live. A change in the paradigm is uncomfortable precisely because it is change. Change requires that we confront mystery. And humans only like mysteries printed in books. But, only in mystery do we find the excitement and awe of discovery. Only in mystery can we truly experience life. Even love itself is a foray into mystery.

As you contemplate your life, always remember that there is another room in the restaurant reserved for those not afraid to try something different. In the end, opening ourselves up to the unknown is less painful than resigning ourselves to the spiritual death of the crab pot.

A Sunday Drive

At the turn of the twenty-first century, there were only seven African Americans serving as CEOs of Fortune 500 companies. One of these men was

Clarence Otis Jr., the CEO of Darden Restaurants, which operates such familiar restaurant chains as Red Lobster, Olive Garden, LongHorn Steakhouse, Bahama Breeze, Seasons 52, The Capital Grille, Eddie V's, and Yard House. Darden is headquartered in Orlando, Florida, and currently employs nearly 200,000 people.

Clarence Otis Jr. is a prime example of someone breaking free from the cage of paradigm. Otis grew up in the Watts ghetto during the civil unrest of the sixties. His father was a janitor for the city of Los Angeles and his mother a homemaker.

Every Sunday, Otis's father would pile the family into the car and drive them roughly twenty miles to the affluent community of Beverly Hills. He didn't do this to engender class hatred or feelings of victimhood, he did this to expand his children's paradigm—to show his children that there was a better world outside of the ghetto. In effect, he was showing them the other room in the restaurant.

It worked. Today, Otis's stellar accomplishments have garnered him recognition, awards, and millions of dollars of compensation. In 2013, Otis was named the eighth-most powerful person in Central Florida by the *Orlando Sentinel.*

The Magic of Imagination

Imagination is more important than
knowledge. For knowledge is limited to
all we now know and understand,
while imagination embraces the entire
world, and all there ever will be
to know and understand.
—ALBERT EINSTEIN

One of the most powerful keys to escaping the cage of paradigm is the power of imagination. Otis climbed out of the ghetto because, with his parents' help, he imagined himself out of it.

Every home in America should have this quote hanging on its wall:

> The success of our lives is more determined by
> our imagination than our circumstance.
>
> —From my book *The Road to Grace*

The power of imagination has been extolled by the greats for centuries. Too few people have been paying attention.

U.S. Route 36 in northern Missouri is a dusty highway stretching from St. Joseph to Hannibal. My daughter and I discovered the route while researching a book I was writing, driving for hours along this boring, uninspiring road. *What a dull spot,* I thought. *What could come from such a place?*

What indeed. Our first day of driving we passed a sign marking the town of Laclede, birthplace of General John Pershing, the highest-ranking military officer in U.S. history. (President Gerald Ford raised George Washington's rank posthumously so that Pershing would not outrank the father of our country.)

We soon discovered that Pershing was just the beginning of a line of great individuals who came from Route 36. We passed Hamilton, Missouri, the birthplace of J. C. Penney; then Marceline, the childhood home of Walt Disney. As an appropriate punctuation, Route 36 ended in Hannibal, Missouri, the imaginary birthplace of Tom Sawyer and the childhood home of Mark Twain.

How was such greatness fostered in such simple locales? How did these great individuals escape the paradigm of small towns, launching their influence on a very big world? *Imagination.* Clearly, they saw beyond the small world of Route 36.

Imagination carries its own magic. J. K. Rowling, the creator of the Harry Potter series, said, "We do not need magic to change the world, we carry all the power we need inside ourselves already: we have the power to imagine better."

And we have the power to act on our imaginations to change our lives.

Starting Points

It might seem obvious, as most great truths are, but *everyone who got to where they are began from where they were.* I know of no one who was born great. Nearly everyone who has changed the world walked a path from obscurity to greatness. In walking our paths of potential, it is important that we do not become overly concerned with where we are, figuratively or literally. The great have always looked not at what is, but what could be. The great look beyond the cage of paradigm.

Marianne Williamson wrote,

Our deepest fear is not that we are inadequate. Our deepest fear is that we are powerful beyond measure. It is our Light, not our Darkness, that most frightens us. We ask ourselves, Who am I to be brilliant, gorgeous, talented, fabulous? Actually, who are you not to be? You are a child of God. Your playing small does not serve the world . . . We were born to make manifest the glory of God that is within us.

This echoes Oprah Winfrey's declaration, "What God intended for you goes far beyond anything you can imagine." Through the power of imagination, the world has been transformed. The same can be true of our inner world.

The True Measure of Greatness

> Greatness does not require a PR firm.

I have found that some people, in searching for a meaningful life, have confused greatness with fame. In spite of our culture's obsession with celebrity, a successful life does not have to include fame and, in most cases, shouldn't. Fame and greatness are not the same thing. There are great people in this world—people of great accomplishment and service to humanity—who are not famous. There are scores of famous people who are not great. In most cases, true greatness is a silent and lonely affair, unaccompanied by the trumpeted fanfare of acclaim.

More important than being known is being of value. The great impact of a loving parent may shake nations. One can only wonder how different the world would be had Adolf Hitler been raised by two kind, happy, and loving parents.

Likewise, the spark lit (or extinguished) by a caring and wise teacher may have saved the world more than once.

To be of value to others is a far greater ambition than the vain hope for the world's fleeting applause and fickle admiration. In the end, it is better to be loved by one person who knows your soul than a million people who don't even know your phone number.

THE CAGE OF VICTIMHOOD

> We can spend our days bemoaning our
> losses, or we can grow from them.
> Ultimately, the choice is ours. We can be
> victims of circumstance or masters of our
> own fate, but make no mistake . . .
> we cannot be both.
> —From my book *The Walk*

We live in a culture of victimhood. Television talk shows parade victims as celebrities. You can hardly drive more than a few miles without encountering some attorney's billboard offering to help you sue someone. Charles J. Sykes, author of the book *A Nation of Victims* (1992), writes that if you add up all the Americans who claim to be victims, they account for more than 400 percent of the population.

The cage of victimhood is seductive for this reason: one can assign all blame to other people or external circumstances and thereby disown any responsibility for one's behavior. Verbally or non-verbally, these caged individuals spout their motto of entitlement with an air of moral superiority, "The world owes me because I have been wronged."

I had just given my "Four Doors" presentation when one of the attendees, a young woman from Texas, approached me.

"I wish my brother had been here. He's the epitome of the victimhood mentality. He's twenty-one and he pretty much just plays videogames in his bedroom all day, living off my mother, even though she has struggled for years to take care of us.

"When anyone tries to talk to him about getting a job, accepting responsibility, or changing his life, he always gives the same answer. He gets angry, then says, 'You don't understand what I'm going through. I'm suffering.'"

"What is he suffering from?" I asked.

"He has ADHD. And my parents divorced."

"That would describe hundreds of thousands of people," I replied.

"Yes, but you can't talk to him about it. He has so completely adopted the role of victim that he's built an impenetrable fortress around himself."

Not a fortress, a *cage.* A fortress may protect one from very real dangers. A cage, ultimately, *is* the danger. This young woman's brother has a character disorder, one that, if he does nothing to address it, will bring great pain and suffering throughout his life. Notwithstanding the very obvious and demonstrable fact that there are millions of people in this world who have suffered far more than this young man has or ever will, he has locked himself up within his own mind and his own contrived victimhood, never even allowing or caring that he contributes nothing to our world and is victimizing others around him. There are none so blind as those who will not see.

While victimhood is not always a choice, the

mentality of victimhood, the reliance on past hurts or injustices to excuse oneself from current responsibility, is. To some degree, everybody suffers. Everybody. The question is not whether or not we have suffered, rather what we have done with our suffering.

I was being interviewed by a newspaper reporter about the problem of victimhood when he said, "Mr. Evans, with all due respect, what do you know about adversity? You're rich and famous."

I was both stunned and a little amused. What he said was partially true: I do have a great life. I have a beautiful family and home. But I also know something about adversity.

One night, when I was twelve years old, I came home late from a friend's house to find the foyer of our home crowded with people. "What's going on?" I asked.

My brother's girlfriend said to me, "Your mother's killed herself."

Shaken, I asked, "Mom's dead?"

"Yes," she replied.

My mother wasn't dead. But she had come close. She had slit her wrists and had been rushed to the hospital. She was kept under psychiatric observation for some time before returning home. After that, she wasn't the same. Whenever she would get upset, she would go to the kitchen and sharpen knives on the electric knife sharpener next to the toaster. The shrill shriek of the knife blades against the sharpening stone would fill the house, sending a message of her intentions. I remember hiding behind the couch, crying and covering my ears against the sound. One night after she had gone to bed, I stole the knife sharpener, wrapped it in towels, and hid it under the sink in the downstairs bathroom.

My mother threatened suicide on many occasions and attempted it twice that I was aware of. One time we came home from church and opened the garage door to find a hose extending from our Nova's exhaust pipe into the running car.

"Dammit," my father said.

"What?" I said, not understanding what I was seeing.

"Are you stupid?" he said. "Your mother's trying to kill herself again."

Suicide wasn't the only form of abandonment I encountered. In fact, my abandonment began at a very young age. One evening when I was in my thirties, I asked my father, "Who raised me when I was an infant?"

He looked at me quizzically. "What do you mean?"

"For years I've heard stories about Mom's deep depression and withdrawal after Sue {my little sister} died. I was only an infant at that time. If she wasn't around, who raised me?"

"We always loved you," my father said, a response that was disturbing in itself.

"I didn't ask that," I said.

"You know I didn't have anything to do with the children," he said.

"Yes, I know," I replied. "So who took care of me?"

He looked at me for a moment, then said, "Pam."

I was stunned. "Who's Pam?"

"She was an unwed teenage mother who was living with us at the time."

This pattern of abandonment repeated itself in different ways throughout my life. When I was ten, I was arguing with my little brother when my mother packed a suitcase, then walked us to the street in front of our home and told us to find some-place else to live. I remember just standing there, suitcase in hand, looking at my brother, who was only seven. "Where are we going to live?" he asked.

I just shook my head. "I don't know."

Two hours later my mother came back out. She was still angry but told us she had changed her mind about kicking us out.

My mother's depression and anxiety were heightened by financial problems. I spent much of my childhood fearful about money, afraid that the police were going to take my parents to jail because we couldn't pay our bills.

It seemed that every time things were improving, something would come along and knock us back down. After losing our home in Arcadia, California, we moved into a moldy, rat-infested house my grandmother had left vacant at her death.

The home was in a blighted part of town, and my siblings and I were exposed to a new world. I was beaten up three times that school year, and my prize possession, a Mickey Mouse watch, was stolen after one of those fights. My sister ran away from home, and my mother lay in bed, sick from her depression, nearly the entire time we lived in that house. I lived in constant anxiety.

Still, things slowly began to improve. My father purchased a lot in a better part of town and our family spent most evenings and weekends building our house. Shortly after moving in, my father, who had taken up construction work, fell on a job site, breaking both of his legs. We had no insurance, no savings, and now, no income. We again lost our home and the ten of us moved into a three-bedroom duplex. I slept on the floor for two years. Decades later, I still clearly remember a man standing at the doorway of our duplex yelling at my mom because we were late on rent. After the confrontation, my mother took to her bed for several days. By the time I left home at the age of nineteen, I had lived in seven different homes.

In addition to these struggles, I grew up with undiagnosed Tourette's syndrome that manifested in several dozen different nervous tics and twitches, both motor and vocal. Because of this, I was ostracized by other children and frequently teased and bullied.

In recounting my past, I'm certain that millions of others in this world have dealt with far greater challenges than mine, but hearing that reporter tell me how easy my life was made me want to laugh out loud.

While it has been immensely valuable for me to identify these early experiences to help me understand how they contributed to my mental map, it is not that old map I choose to operate from today. I sought to understand my past only so I could use that information to identify the false roads and routes I had created to survive at a very different and vulnerable time of life—and then change them.

The Twin Problems of Victimhood

There are two primary obstacles to growth, freedom, and happiness that come from the victimhood mentality. First, as demonstrated by the young man who locked himself in his bedroom, embracing victimhood takes away our freedom of self-determination by giving control of our lives to some other person or external circumstance or event.

Let me be clear. I'm not saying that you're not

a victim or haven't been wronged. *Everyone who has walked the planet has, in some way, been wronged.* As such, the question to ask ourselves is not "Have I been injured?" but "Do I want to define my life by my injuries?"

Life's greatest gifts often come wrapped in adversity.

—From my book *Finding Noel*

The second primary danger of the victimhood mentality is that it ignores the reality that most of the greatest learning experiences of our lives come from our adversities. In many cases, we do not succeed in spite of our challenges and difficulties, but precisely because of them.

In my early twenties, I worked at a small advertising agency in Salt Lake City. One of our clients was a local radio station. At the station's request, I designed a billboard campaign featuring the station's radio hosts. One of the boards was to be a picture of their popular morning drive host sticking out his tongue, beneath the words:

MAGIC 107.5.

HOME OF MARK'S GOLDEN TONGUE

The station approved the campaign, and the next week the DJ met me at a photography studio to take his picture. To my dismay, I discovered that the DJ was unable to stick his tongue out past his lips.

"When I was eighteen months old," the host said, "I drank Drano and I had to take speech therapy to learn to speak normal."

"You don't just speak *normal*," I said. "You've got a golden tongue."

"You know how it is," he replied. "Our weaknesses become our strengths."

History bears record of this principle. Wilma Rudolph was born prematurely, weighing just four and a half pounds at birth, and the twentieth of twenty-two children. At the age of four she contracted polio and had to wear a brace and corrective shoes for most of her childhood. But Rudolph had no desire to live life handicapped. Through physical therapy, incredible devotion, and hard work, she not only overcame her disability but went on to compete in two Olympic Games in track and field. She was the first American woman to win three gold medals at a single Olympic Games, and during the 1960s she was considered to be the fastest woman in the world.

Another stellar example of the rejection of victimhood was Helen Keller. Keller was born in 1880 as a normal healthy child. When she was nineteen months old, she contracted an illness that left her deaf and blind. Through the help of a gifted teacher, Anne Sullivan, Helen learned to communicate and went on to become a prolific writer, publishing twelve books and several articles.

Lessons from the Vineyard

A decade ago, I took my family to live in the Chianti region of Italy, home of some of the most revered wines and vineyards in the world. Every day I would look out our bedroom window and see the beautiful rolling hills ripe with blushing grapes and think, *Sembra una cartolina*—It looks just like a postcard.

During our time in Italy, I became friends with a local winemaker. On one occasion, I said to him, "Chianti must have very fertile soil to produce such famous grapes." His reply surprised me. "No," he said. "We have terrible soil. Good grapes do not grow in good soil."

I did some research on this. It turns out that grapes are lazy. If the soil they grow in is too fertile, the grapes do not need to extend their roots deeply, which results in mediocre grapes that are used to make cheap table wine.

Because the soil in Chianti is poor, the grapevines develop large, intricate root systems that stretch deep into the ground, extracting not only what they need to survive but many other nutrients and minerals as well. The result is a sweet, delicious grape.

The metaphor is obvious and thought-provoking. A biologist once said to me, "I have noticed that in nature things with easy lives tend to die young."

Living with Tourette's Syndrome

At the age of forty-one, I was diagnosed with Tourette's syndrome—not that I hadn't suspected it earlier. The powerful impulses I felt to stand up and shout profanities in public places or to spit in the faces of important people always struck me as a bit peculiar. (Thankfully, I never succumbed to those impulses.) Still, hearing the diagnosis of Tourette's from a doctor had a powerful impact on me.

"You mean you didn't know you had Tourette's?" the doctor asked.

I shook my head. "I knew something was wrong, but I just thought I was a little odd."

Then something peculiar happened. I began to cry. Not a little cry, but a deep sob that rose up from my belly with force. For several minutes I wept. Not for me or for my life—I have a great life—but for that lonely little boy who endured years of isolation, anxiety, and teasing.

Tourette's syndrome is a particularly difficult disorder for children to experience, as it oftentimes brings estrangement and ridicule. I constantly wondered why I couldn't be normal like the other kids. I remember on many occasions hiding my tics from others or holding my face, hoping the tics would stop. During my first (and only) summer camp, I was surrounded by a group of children who wanted to see my tics. One of them shouted, "Let's see what the freak does next."

As I sat there crying in the doctor's office, the wise doctor said, "Richard, your Tourette's is a gift."

I looked up, angry at his comment. "You call this a gift?"

"Do you know why I'm seeing you?" he asked.

I thought it was an odd question. "Because I made an appointment," I replied.

"No," he said. "I'm primarily a researcher. I don't take patients. But when a colleague of mine told me that she suspected you had Tourette's, I wanted to see if I could help, after what you did for me."

"We've never met," I said. "What have I done for you?"

"More than you can imagine," he replied. "Several years ago, my wife and I lost a child. As difficult as it was for me, my wife took it even harder, and I wondered if she would ever recover. It was one of your books that helped her through her pain and emotionally brought her back. In return, I wanted to somehow help you."

Then he said something especially thought provoking. "Do you think it's a coincidence that you write the books you do, filled with such compassion and empathy, and you have Tourette's?" He shook his head. "No, you write the way you do precisely because you have Tourette's."

I have considered that wise doctor's words many times. If I were given the option to magically choose a life without Tourette's but I had to give up the lessons and strengths that came from my disability, I wouldn't do it. I would choose to have the Tourette's.

I've learned that I'm not alone in such feelings. I had just finished speaking at the Los Angeles book festival at UCLA when a man approached me.

"Mr. Evans, I really liked what you said about adversity. I would like to share something with you.

"We have been conducting a rather interesting study. We've surveyed more than a thousand people struggling with different handicaps. We asked them this question, 'If I had a pill that could take away your handicap, but will make you lose everything you have gained from your adversity, would you take the pill?'" He looked me in the eyes. "Guess how many people have taken the pill."

I was thinking of a number in the ninety percent range but answered, "Seventy-five percent?"

He shook his head. "Let me ask you this: Would you take the pill?"

I thought a moment, then said, "No."

He smiled. "Neither would anyone else. No one has taken the pill."

Amy

I was signing books in northern Utah when I noticed a beautiful young girl with a pronounced tic standing in line next to her mother. (One of the characteristics of Tourette's syndrome is that those who have it are usually easy to spot.) When the girl and her mother got to the signing table, I asked the little girl her name.

"Amy," she said.

"Amy, may I tell you a secret?" I asked.

She looked up at her mother, then back at me. "Yes."

I leaned close to her and whispered, "I have Tourette's syndrome."

Her eyes grew wide. Then she leaned forward and whispered back, "So do I!"

"Isn't it great?" I said.

She looked perplexed. "It is?"

"I know it doesn't seem like it now, but someday you'll find all these wonderful parts of yourself that you have because of your Tourette's."

I looked up and saw tears streaming down the mother's face. "Thank you," she mouthed.

The Power of Forgiveness

The ship releases its anchor not for the
anchor's benefit, but for the ship.

The very antithesis of the victimhood mentality
is the attitude of forgiveness. In today's strike-
back culture, forgiveness is poorly understood. All
too often we withhold forgiveness and cling to
our wrongs as if they were some kind of treasure.
They're not. Still, I've met people who have
held on to their grudges decades after the focus
of their resentment is dead and buried. What these
people fail to recognize is that forgiveness does less
for the forgiven than the forgiver. To release the
chains of resentment brings freedom.

I invite you to try an experiment I've shared
with thousands of people around the world. Before
you turn the page, take just a moment, close your
eyes, and ask God who it is you need to forgive. See
if a name comes to your mind. (If your initial re-

sponse is "No, not them! Anyone but them!" then you can be especially sure that you've got the right name.)

Then forgive them. If it is impossible to forgive them face-to-face, do it by phone or letter. If they are no longer living, declare your forgiveness out loud to the universe.

The person you're forgiving might not accept your forgiveness. Being told, or reminded, that they've wronged you might even anger them. But remember, you're not doing it for *them,* you're doing it for *you.* And, no matter their response, you won't be the same afterward. You'll have taken a critical step toward personal freedom.

The Justice of Self-Forgiveness

Many times the most difficult individual to forgive is yourself. In a bizarre act of injustice, we try ourselves over and over for the same crime. There's a legal term for this: double jeopardy. And it was considered to be an act of such injustice that the founding fathers specifically added it as the Fifth Amendment of the Constitution.

"{N}or shall any person be subject for the same offense to be twice put in jeopardy of life or limb . . ."

The goal of the double jeopardy amendment is to avoid a retrial after an acquittal or a conviction, and multiple punishments for the same crime.

Yet that is precisely what we do to ourselves. We try ourselves over and over for the same offense, then inflict repeated punishments of self-hate, guilt, and rejection. This is wholly unjust and ethically wrong.

There is nothing wrong with feeling guilt for the things we do wrong. But once we have identified and confessed our mistake and, if possible, tried to make amends for it, the just and honest thing to do is to let it go. We all make mistakes. Holding on to past wrongs is as foolish as a basketball player perseverating over a missed shot in a previous game. It not only distracts from the current game but increases the chance of repeating the mistake.

As if justice wasn't already enough of a reason, there is another important reason for self-forgiveness. Oftentimes we specifically attack others for the crimes we are unable to forgive in ourselves. Therefore, the act of forgiving ourselves opens us up to the possibility of forgiving others.

Here are two exercises to help you mentally overcome the anguish of personally inflicted double jeopardy.

First, the next time a thought of self-incrimination pops into your mind over something you've already suffered for, call it out. Identify the exact offense, when it took place, and how many times you've punished yourself for the error. (You may have to estimate—the number may be in the hundreds or thousands.) Then say to yourself, *"I know that I did wrong, but I've already paid for my mistake. Punishing myself over and over for what I've already suffered is unjust to me and God. I hereby finally forgive myself and let it go forever."*

The thought may come again, but it will be weaker the next time. Call it out each time it comes until it completely vanishes.

Second, if you are still dealing with a recent indiscretion and doing your best to make amends, then try repeating this mantra until you feel peace:

I have done wrong,
I confess it to Thee.
I seek Thy correction,
To be more like Thee.

While these techniques have worked powerfully for me, you might want to create your own ritual, such as visualizing your wrongdoing as a balloon and letting it go, or lighting a candle and blowing it out, etc.

The important thing is the recognition of the injustice of self-inflicted double jeopardy and ending the mental loop that continues to bring you pain.

The Power of Gratitude

One of the greatest indicators of someone who has embraced the victimhood mentality is their utter lack of gratitude. "What do I have to be grateful for?" they whine. To admit gratitude is to upset the creaky platform on which they've built their cage. For this reason alone, gratitude is one of the greatest antidotes to the victimhood mentality.

Begin your escape to freedom by denouncing victimhood and make a list of everything good that has come, or may come, from your struggles. Write down what you are most grateful for.

Changing your map may take time. But remember, freedom is not measured in totality, but degrees. Every step toward freedom will bring you more joy, contentment, and peace.

A Father's Letter to His Son

This is a letter from my book *A Winter Dream* that I gave to my own son:

Always, always remember that adversity is not a detour. It is part of the path.

You will encounter obstacles. You will make mistakes. Be grateful for both. Your obstacles and mistakes will be your greatest teachers. And the only way to not make mistakes in this life is to do nothing, which is the biggest mistake of all.

Your challenges, if you let them, will become your greatest allies. Mountains can crush or raise you, depending on which side of the mountain you choose to stand on. All history bears out that the great, those who have changed the world, have all suffered great challenges. And, more times than not, it's precisely those challenges that, in God's time, lead to triumph.

Abhor victimhood. Denounce entitlement. Neither are gifts, rather cages to damn the soul. Everyone who has walked this earth is a victim of injustice. Everyone.

Most of all, do not be too quick to denounce your sufferings. The difficult road you are called to walk may, in fact, be your only path to success.

Everyone has problems. It's how we choose to deal with our problems that matters. Some people choose to be whiners—some choose to be winners. Some choose to be victims—some choose to be victors.

I'm not suggesting that you deny the existence of past injustices and hurts; rather I'm advocating a radical and liberating change of attitude toward those injustices and hurts. Stop using past pain as currency to buy out of present living.

In the end, the victimhood mentality simply is not worth it. It isolates its prisoners from joy, freedom, and meaningful relationships. Initially, it might be frightening to leave the dank shelter of the victimhood cage, but it's the only way to fly.

THE CAGE OF FEAR

> The greatest shackles we wear in this life
> are those forged of our own fears.
> —From my book *The Looking Glass*

Fear is a blessing. It's a basic survival mechanism that has served and protected humankind for thousands of years. Fear can also be an unhealthy and enslaving flaw in our mental maps.

The difference between healthy and unhealthy fear is appropriateness. Fearing a charging lion, a speeding car, or a coiled rattlesnake is an appropriate, healthy and, perhaps, lifesaving response. Fearing a cotton ball isn't. Yet people do fear cotton balls—figuratively as well as literally.

Psychologists have long known that specific fears can be learned or conditioned. In a controversial (and blatantly unethical) experiment conducted in 1920, psychologist John Watson demonstrated empirically that fear was not only a natural, unconditioned response to danger but could be conditioned to nondangerous stimuli as well. In a famous case study called the Little Albert experiment, Watson conditioned a nine-month-old boy to fear a white rat, then extended that phobia to other harmless objects.

A close friend of mine has a phobia of snakes. While it is natural, common and, in some cases, healthy to fear some snakes, her fear is extreme. Once, while driving on the freeway at more than seventy miles an hour, she nearly swerved off the road because there was a snake crawling on it. Had her husband not grabbed the wheel, she might have killed both of them.

In this instance, her fear was far more dangerous than the object of her fear. When I asked her if she knew why she was so afraid of snakes, she shared with me a memory of being chased with a rattlesnake held by an adult who should have been protecting her.

Irrational fear is hardly unusual. While no one I know has ever been killed—or even hurt—speaking in public, many people fear standing before an audience nearly as much as they do death. In addressing this cage, the two types of fear I'm specifically referring to are the *fear of pain* and the *fear of failure*.

The Fear of Pain

While the fear of pain is a natural and primal response, it can also be easily conditioned to stunt our personal growth and happiness. If a child is bitten by a dog, she may choose to avoid dogs or run away should she encounter one. But not all dogs bite. And to resist all dogs is to deny the loving companionship a dog might provide. Taken to an extreme, this fear could bring her daily anxiety.

The truest sign of life is growth. And growth requires pain. So to choose life is, to some extent, to accept pain. Still, many reject this fact—which is as pointless as renouncing the law of gravity. They complain and whine as if their pain was an aberration of the natural and only correct state of affairs. In the extreme, these people may go to such lengths to avoid pain that they give up on life. They bury their hearts, or they drug themselves with narcotics or alcohol until they don't feel anything anymore. The cruel irony is that, in the end, their attempted escape from pain becomes more painful than the pain they're fleeing.

The Fear of Failure

In a way, the fear of failure is just another manifestation of the fear of pain. To fail is to hurt. Whether we have failed in business or a relationship, pain is the cost of that failure. Indeed, if failure wasn't painful, we probably wouldn't fear it.

To fly we must first accept the possibility of falling.

—From my book *The Walk*

Removing emotional pain from failure requires two things. First, we must learn to separate our identities from our temporary circumstances. We may fail at achieving a specific goal, but that does not alter our inherent state of being or divinity. Just because things don't seem to be going our way doesn't mean that we are any less valuable or important. Humanity is sometimes at its very best in its lulls: its darkest or lowest moments.

We can stop berating ourselves when we don't hit the target, and, instead, use the experience to adjust our aim. Not surprisingly, this will not only take away the self-hate and criticism that is usually the greatest part of failure's pain, but will get us closer to our goals. It is up to you to change your identity from "failure" to "scientist" or "explorer."

The second secret to removing the pain from failure is to view failure realistically—not as a contrived finale or absolute state, but rather as a requisite step toward a larger objective. This requires that we change our self-talk from absolutism to experimentalism—the language of scientists. Edison, Ford, Marconi, and the Wright brothers each had myriad "failures" before reaching their end goals. Yet it is difficult to term these early experiments as failures, as each experiment advanced the scientist's cause toward his final objective. It is fortunate for all of us that these innovators viewed temporary failures not as *an end,* but rather as *part of the process toward an end.*

Edison exhibited the perfect experimental attitude. When the media criticized him for his failure to create the incandescent lightbulb by the deadline he had publicly announced, Edison responded, "I have not failed. I've just found ten thousand ways that won't work." Today, Edison's successful light-bulb is the very symbol of a good idea.

Where did we learn that failure was shameful? Thomas J. Watson, the chairman and CEO of IBM, said, "Would you like me to give you a formula for success? It's quite simple, really. *Double your rate of failure.* You are thinking of failure as the enemy of success. But it isn't at all. You can be discouraged by failure—or you can learn from it. So go ahead and make mistakes. Make all you can. Because, remember, that's where you will find success."

Scottish author Samuel Smiles said, "It is a mistake to suppose that men succeed through success; they much oftener succeed through failures. Precept, study, advice, and example could never have taught them so well as failure has done." And Emerson wrote, "Do not be too timid and squeamish about your actions. All life is an experiment. The more experiments you make the better."

The Failure That Fails

Inaction due to the fear of failure
is failure.

My own life experience has taught me that it's okay to fail, but it's not okay to not try. There have been times in my life when I so feared the risk of failure that I effectively, if not passively, embraced it. This is all too common behavior. The thinking of a *passive failure* goes like this:

I'd like to get a raise. But if I ask for one, I might not get it and I might make my boss mad. Better to not try.

So we don't ask and the guaranteed result is no raise.

I learned a powerful lesson about passive failure from a young woman named Heather Williams.

Heather Williams was the most beautiful girl in the ninth grade at Bonneville Junior High School. I'll never forget the first time I saw Heather. It was the last week of school, and I was sitting on a school bus about to go on an end-of-the-year field trip, when she walked onto the bus.

I just gaped. I had never seen anyone so beautiful in my life. I turned to the guy sitting next to me. "Who is that?"

"Heather Williams," he said. "She just moved here." Then he added, "She's way out of your league."

Of course she was out of my league. She was perfection. I was . . . me. But I was also a dreamer. I dreamed about Heather all summer. I wondered what she was like. I wondered what it would be like to have her as my girlfriend. I wondered what it would be like to kiss her.

Summer ended and a new school year began.

On my first day of high school, I went to my third-period class and sat down in the middle of a row of empty seats. A few minutes later, Heather Williams walked into the room. She looked around the room and then, to my surprise, walked over and sat down at the desk next to mine.

It took me a while to get up the nerve to talk to her. But after three days, I learned that Heather was not only beautiful on the outside but on the inside as well. In a moment of rare optimism, I decided that I was going to ask her to the homecoming dance.

Every day for the next two weeks, I struggled to summon the courage to ask her out, only to lose it when she walked in the door. Finally, on a Sunday night just a few weeks before the dance, I faced the fact that I was running out of time and committed myself. *Tomorrow's the day,* I thought. *I'm asking Heather Williams to Homecoming.*

Monday morning as I walked to school, I told another student about my plan to ask Heather to the dance. "You're too late," he said. "She's already been asked."

My heart fell. "Who asked her?"

"Tom Watts," he replied.

Every high school in America has a Tom Watts. Tom Watts had perfect skin and golden hair with just a hint of curl. He was the cocaptain of the sophomore football team. All the girls loved Tom Watts.

I assuaged my disappointment with feigned relief. *Dodged that bullet,* I thought. *That kid was right. Heather Williams was way out of my league.*

Throughout the rest of high school, I never fully lost my crush on Heather. My mouth would go dry when I'd see her in the hall or at lunch. I voted for her when she was elected as senior prom royalty. But my dream was gone. I never went out with Heather Williams. I never kissed Heather Williams. I never even held her hand.

School ended. I didn't see Heather again until ten years later, at our high school class reunion.

Still beautiful, I thought. She smiled when she saw me. We talked a long while about high school and what had happened in our lives since graduation. Then, as we were about to part, she said, "Do you know what vexed me most about high school?"

"What?" I asked.

"That you never once asked me out. You probably don't remember, but we sat next to each other in third period of our sophomore year. I had the biggest crush on you."

Someone kill me, I thought. My dream was just waiting for me to claim it. Instead, I had listened to my fear and received its reward.

I vowed that I would never passively choose failure again; that I would rather fail in a burst of flame than rust to death in obscurity. At least a fireball provided some illumination to the world.

Even in failure, we rarely regret what we attempt. We nearly always regret what we don't.

Summary

Paradigm. Victimhood. Fear. Since these three cages exist entirely in our minds, it may seem that it is entirely up to us to liberate ourselves from ourselves.

It's not. We are not alone in our quest for freedom. The work of spiritual liberation is the work of God. Asking for Divine assistance to free ourselves from destructive and flawed mental maps is a powerful and, arguably, necessary first step. God witnessed the tangling of our lives; He knows how to untie them.

If this sounds familiar, it should. This principle correlates with six of the twelve steps of Alcoholics Anonymous. Turning our lives over to a greater power is, perhaps, the most sure way to discover the divinity of our lives.

DOOR THREE

Magnify Your Life

Magnify Your Life

To magnify a life is to expand its influence and power beyond its current realm. It means to push and explore the limits of our divine potential. To magnify our lives also means to exchange our mental maps with much larger ones.

DREAMING

We cannot live what we cannot dream.

When my youngest daughter was in the third grade, to commemorate Martin Luther King Jr. Day, her teacher gave each of the students in her class a piece of paper with the words "I have a dream . . ." written on top. The students were given the assignment to write in their own visions for a better world. When my daughter showed me her paper, I smiled. Below the words "I have a dream," she had written:

> *That someday handicap people will be able to park wherever they want.*

I was pleased that she had been given the assignment. I've always been a dreamer. When I was nine years old, picking up discarded nails on a construction site for thirty-five cents an hour, I dreamed of being wealthy.

When I was sweeping out the basement of the school my dad was working on, covered with dust and gypsum powder, I dreamed of being someone important in politics.

Watching other guys at school talking confidently with girls, I dreamed of someday having a beautiful wife.

When famed explorer John Goddard presented an assembly at my school, I dreamed of traveling the world and experiencing other countries and cultures.

In the fifth grade, my science teacher showed us how the poles on magnets attracted or repelled each other and told us that if we invented a way to make a motor run from these magnets he'd give us five hundred dollars. (Actually, what he was proposing—a perpetual motion motor—would be worth billions.)

I dreamed that I could create such a motor, and, using the magnets from the back of plastic refrigerator letters, I spent the next two weeks building more than a dozen prototypes before finally giving up.

Like I said, I have always been a dreamer. And all of my dreams (except for a working perpetual motion motor) have come true. *All of them.* I have been blessed with a remarkable life. I have traveled more than a million miles, visiting all but three of the fifty states, and more than twenty countries. My beautiful wife and I have danced in the White House and dined with presidents and prime ministers. I have sat with governors and U.S. senators in hotel suites watching election returns come in. I have sold millions of copies of my books in dozens of languages and have received tens of thousands of letters from people whose lives have been touched by those books. My charity has helped more than fifty thousand abused or neglected children. I believe that none of these things could have happened had I not dreamed big when my life was so small.

Dreaming is the first step in magnifying our

lives. I believe that once we begin to focus on a dream, our mind, and perhaps the universe, draws our desire to us. While this reeks of magical thinking, I believe there is something to it. One year I wrote down that I wished to travel to China. Four months later, a friend called to tell me that she had just won a trip for two to China and her husband had no interest in going. She asked if my wife and I would like to go. The trip was life-changing for us, for a few years later, we adopted a little girl from Guangdong Province.

THE "WHAT IF?" QUESTION

One of the devices that novelists use in creating a story is to ask the "what if" question. You might recognize some of these "what ifs."

What if a young boy finds out that he's really a powerful wizard? *What if* a teenage girl moves to a small town and falls in love with a boy she discovers is really a vampire? *What if* a young Italian man falls in love with a woman he learns is a member of his family's town rivals?

The "what if" exercise is a useful device in creating real-life stories as well. Making your own list of "what ifs" is a powerful way to begin to alter your mental map to magnify your life.

> *What if* I went back to school and studied art history?
>
> *What if* I changed my sedentary lifestyle and became a competitive cyclist?
>
> *What if* I wrote that book I've always dreamed about? *What if* it became a bestseller?

A little more than a decade ago my wife came to me with a completely unexpected and, at the time, absurd "what if?" *What if we just picked up our family and moved to Italy for a year?*

Incredibly, five months later we did just that.

The result was a better marriage, a closer family, a broader worldview for our children, and wonderful, happy memories we will always cherish.

Start making your own list of "what ifs." Make them the most fulfilling, exciting "what ifs" you can imagine. Think about how they might affect your life. Then ask yourself, "Why not?"

TAKING RISKFUL ACTION

> Life is either a daring adventure or
> nothing. Security does not exist in nature,
> nor do the children of men as a whole
> experience it. Avoiding danger is no safer
> in the long run than exposure.
> —HELEN KELLER

The second step to magnifying our lives is the by-product of escaping the cage of fear. Take risks. Life, by definition, *is a risk.* I am grateful for the great risks I have taken in my life—even the ones that ended up badly.

> You miss 100 percent of the
> shots you don't take.
> —WAYNE GRETZKY

As I wrote before, we rarely regret our failed attempts, but we nearly always regret the ones we don't take. One of my personal favorite *risk* experiences is one I call "taking the seat."

TAKING THE SEAT

When I first entered the publishing world, it was a lot different than it is today. There were no ebooks. In fact, there were almost no books sold on the Internet. Chain bookstores were still unheard of in many parts of the country, and, for the most part, the book industry consisted of thousands of small, independent bookstores—the so-called mom-and-pop stores of yesteryear.

This bookselling landscape presented a nearly insurmountable challenge to a writer like me: a new unheard-of author who didn't have the backing of a major publisher.

To get my first book into bookstores, I traveled around the country to regional book shows. This was both time-consuming and expensive, but I believed in my book and wanted to push my dream as far and as high as I could.

The September before my book was to come out, I flew to Denver to the Mountains and Plains book show hoping to introduce my books to regional booksellers. I rented a small booth, then sat behind a table looking for booksellers, identifiable by their red badges.

Unfortunately, after several hours few booksellers had walked by. I sought out one of the show's organizers to find out where all the booksellers were.

"They're with the authors," she replied. "In Hall B."

I walked over to the adjacent conference hall. Sure enough, there were hundreds of booksellers in roped-off lines, waiting their turn to get a free signed book from one of the bestselling authors sitting at the front of the room.

How do I compete with that? I said to myself.

As I stood there wondering what to do, I noticed that there was an empty seat at the author's table. A little voice said to me, "You want to be a bestselling author? Take the seat."

There was no way I was going to take the seat. There were "guards" up there. They'd throw me out.

As I turned to walk away, justifiably resigned to the unfairness of the situation (victim mentality), that small inner voice said to me, "How much do you care about your book? If you're not willing to fight for your dreams, who will?"

The words hit me hard. Before I could talk myself out of it, I went back to my booth, grabbed a box of my books, and returned to the crowded hall. I climbed the dais, set my box down on the table, and sat down between two bestselling authors.

Someone noticed. Out of the corner of my eye I saw one of the show personnel making a beeline toward me. When she got to my side, I looked up and said, "Sorry I'm late."

The woman just stared at me for a moment then said, "May I get you some water?"

"That would be great," I said.

I sat there for the rest of the session handing out my little book to hundreds of booksellers.

The next year my book was a *New York Times* bestseller and one of the most talked-about books of the season. My publisher sent me out on a book tour, and I was invited back to that same trade show in Denver. Only this time I had an entourage: my agent, my publicist, and my publisher's representative. I was not only listed on the show's program, but on the cover of it as well.

As I walked up on the stage in the very same conference hall, I recognized the woman from the year before. As she walked up to me, I asked her if she knew who I was.

"Of course, Mr. Evans," she replied. "Everyone here knows who you are."

"That's not what I meant," I said. "Do you remember me from last year?"

Her eyes suddenly lit with recognition. "You're the guy who crashed the book signing!"

I smiled. "That's me."

"Congratulations," she said. "You made it."

"Thanks for not throwing me out," I said.

"I was going to," she said. "That's my job. But when you looked up at me, I just couldn't bring myself to do it." She smiled, then said, "May I get you some water?"

• • •

I love that story. Not just because it happened to me or because I'm a sucker for happy endings, but because it illustrates perfectly what life asks of us. You want to be happy? Take the seat. You want freedom? Take the seat. You want a meaningful life? Take the seat.

WORK

> Faith, without works, is dead.
> —JAMES 2:17

Cultures expose their core beliefs through their stories and parables. At one time, industry and hard work was a favorite American cultural theme. Growing up, everyone I knew was familiar with the stories of "The Ant and the Grasshopper" and "The Little Red Hen." Sadly, these stories extolling the virtue of hard work have all but disappeared. Or maybe they have just been updated and our culture's gladiators have taken up the torch. I've yet to hear a successful college athlete attribute his or her success to slacking off or practicing less. Nor do I ever expect to.

There is currently much debate on whether Americans (specifically American children) are becoming increasingly lazy. Frankly, I have nothing to contribute to the debate, and statistics can be wielded to defend both sides of the argument. What I do know is that those who have changed the world have always given credit to hard work.

To work hard is to work with directed passion toward accomplishing an objective, not just punching a clock. It means to give and do more than is expected of you.

A strong work ethic was considered an important virtue in my family. My father outwardly prided himself on his ability to work harder than men younger than him and boasted that he and his boys could outwork any crew on the construction site. But I encountered many on job sites who felt differently. These men gave as little to their employers as they could get away with. Somewhere in their mentality was the mindset that they were in conflict with their employer and the less they gave, the more they "won."

This is folly. The physical world does not reward sloth. On my first job on a political campaign, my direct supervisor prided himself on how adept he was at delegating his work to others. He loaded me up with everything he didn't want to do. I didn't complain; I just did my best to get everything done. Within three months, he was dismissed, and I was given his job.

When my first book became a number-one bestseller, I heard repeated comments on how lucky I was. Of course I was. But, as Thomas Jefferson said, "I'm a great believer in luck, and I find the harder I work the more I have of it."

What I rarely heard commented on were the months I spent on the road promoting my book, the lost sleep and countless mornings getting up at 3 A.M. for east coast radio interviews, the thousands of sales pitches and signed books. For two years, I was passionately focused on success and worked constantly to make it happen. By the time my first book hit a bestsellers list, I was exhausted.

THE POWER OF CONSISTENT EFFORT

I believe that most of our successes are to be found in the margins of our lives. Almost all of the successful authors I know wrote their first books while working other demanding jobs. Few people realize how much of their lives are wasted or how much just a little extra effort could pay off.

I believe it's not so much laziness that saps the power of our lives as it is poor planning. Just 10 minutes a day of loving service to your spouse could vastly improve the other 1,430 minutes. Just 60 minutes a week of one-on-one time with a child could powerfully affect the other 10,020.

Small actions done with consistency can net huge results. For instance, I've met people who wish they were better read but complain that they just don't have the time. Consider this. If you were to consistently read just ten pages a day, in one year you could read:

The Great Gatsby
Madame Bovary
The Adventures of Huckleberry Finn
The Crucible
Brave New World
Animal Farm
On Liberty
1984
Beowulf
. . . And the complete works of William Shakespeare

Great things can happen in the margins of your day and the spare moments of your life.

WORKING WITH PASSION

**I know you've heard it a thousand times
before. But it's true—hard work pays off.
If you want to be good, you have to
practice, practice, practice. If you don't
love something, then don't do it.**
— Ray Bradbury

When I was little, my older brothers used to tell me that I was lazy, which, considering our family's work ethic, was a hurtful slur. For years I believed them. It was only after I entered the external work force that I learned otherwise. The manager at my first real job, at a TacoTime, told me he wished that every one of his employees worked as hard as I did. I began to hear this at every job I took. It really struck home when a business partner of mine said, "I think you might be the hardest-working man I have ever met."

The truth was, I was never really lazy. I was

just young, and my brothers would give me the jobs that they didn't want—mundane, boring tasks like picking up scrap wood or gathering nails, nothing I could ever truly be passionate about. That's not to say I didn't work hard at these tasks, but psychologically, how long can one remain motivated and excited doing something one doesn't like?

> Without passion we are doomed to mediocrity.
> —From my book *The Locket*

One of the secrets of being a hard worker is to find jobs with objectives you care about. Of course you won't like every aspect of any job, but if you are passionate enough about the cause, it's easy to project a powerful work ethic through the tasks you dislike.

Summary

When I consider how my light is spent
Ere half my days,
in this dark world and wide,
And that one Talent,
which is death to hide,
Lodg'd with me useless,
though my Soul more bent
To serve therewith my Maker, and present
My true account, lest he, returning, chide
—JOHN MILTON

One of the better-known Bible stories is the parable of the talents in the book of Matthew. In this story a wealthy man entrusts each of his three servants with talents—valuable gold coins—to care for in his absence. The first two servants wisely use the talents to create more wealth. The third servant, "fearful" of losing his one talent, buries his in the ground.

When the master returns he is pleased with the first two servants and promises them great joy. But he is angry with the third servant, relinquishing him to darkness and weeping. Regret.

This is a fitting metaphor of the Third Door. To magnify our lives is to take those talents and gifts unique to each of us and with them, utilizing imagination, risk, work and consistent effort, make more out of our lives. As the parable promises, in this we will find great joy.

DOOR FOUR

Develop a Love-Centered Map

Develop a Love-Centered Map

Love is the ultimate and highest goal
to which man can aspire.
—VIKTOR E. FRANKL

At the age of twenty-three, I experienced a spiritual eclipse. I was struggling with marriage, life, depression, and a feeling of being abandoned by God. I was constantly fighting suicidal thoughts—a common phenomenon among children with a suicidal parent.

At the time, I was working as a copywriter at a small advertising agency. One afternoon I noticed that our company receptionist was reading a book called *Return from Tomorrow.* I picked it up and read a few pages, then asked if I could borrow it.

"Take it," she said. "I just finished it."

I carried the book up into my office, locked the door, and read the entire book from cover to cover.

The book, written by psychiatrist Dr. George G. Ritchie, is about the near-death experience he had at the age of twenty while serving in the military during World War II. Dr. Ritchie was legally dead for nine minutes and was even given a death certificate and carried out of his hospital room in a body bag. (It was this book that later inspired Dr. Raymond Moody's research into near-death experiences and his subsequent book *Life After Life.*)

I couldn't stop reading the book. Not only did it seem to answer all the questions I was struggling with in my life at that time, I felt a remarkable sense of peace as I read it. Something about it just felt right—almost as if I were remembering something I already knew. Almost immediately I began feeling better and closer to God.

Five years later, I had just published my first book and was at a book show to promote it when I read in the program that Dr. Ritchie was one of the guest speakers. The book *Embraced by the Light* by Betty J. Eadie (another book about a near-death experience) was the number-one nonfiction book in the country at the time, and the show organizers had brought together a panel of authors with similar books.

I attended the discussion and found Dr. Ritchie just as interesting and credible in person as he was in his book. I desperately wanted to meet him. After the session, I rushed up from the back of the room as his handlers were leading him out.

"Dr. Ritchie," I shouted across the stage. "Your book changed my life."

He turned back and looked at me with a warm, intrigued expression, then said, "For the better, I hope."

His escort stepped between us. "Mr. Ritchie

has a book signing," she said flatly as she led him out of the room.

I walked down to the author hall where Dr. Ritchie was to be signing books, only to find his table vacant. I was terribly disappointed. I really felt that I needed to meet him. As I walked back to the main hall, someone tapped me on the shoulder. It was Dr. Ritchie. "We need to talk," he said.

We found a quiet place to sit. He told me that the booksellers had lost his books so he had nothing to sign, but he'd stayed because he felt a strong need to find me. For the next hour, we talked about his experience in death, modern religion, and the nature of God. After our conversation, I was even more convinced of the authenticity of his experience. I also genuinely loved the man for his courageous honesty and the hope he had shared with me and the world.

We kept in touch. He and his wife visited me in Salt Lake City, and I had the pleasure of being his guest as he spoke to a large local audience.

The part of Dr. Ritchie's book that had hit me the hardest was his description of meeting God and the questions God asked him. The ultimate question God asked was "Did you learn to love?"

Dr. Ritchie wrote that he had felt like a student who had come to a final exam only to discover he would be tested on a subject he had never studied. In the deepest recess of my heart, I understood what he was saying, as I would have felt the same way. I suspect many of us would. Too many of us have been studying for the wrong exam. In the end, there is no earthly award, medal, résumé, or bank account large enough to impress God—only an accounting of how we loved His children. I believe, as Socrates wrote, that it is only through love that we approach the Divine.

Whether you accept the reality of Dr. Ritchie's experience or not, it is difficult to refute that love is the secret to joy. I've lived long enough to know that the greatest source of my happiness comes from giving and receiving love.

Even though the world downplays and distorts the nature and importance of love, that does not diminish the fact that love is a need. Without love, infants die. Emotionally, so do adults. With love, our health improves, both physically and emotionally. But what is love?

A DEFINITION OF LOVE

The task of defining love is one that some of humanity's greatest minds have wrestled with for millennia. Philosophers, spiritualists, theologians, and psychologists have all contributed their explanations of the phenomenon.

For the purpose of this book, I sought a definition that would best serve our objective of creating a love-centered map. I found a pretty good definition while living in Florence, Italy.

One Sunday afternoon, a young Italian woman who had befriended our family smiled at me, then said, "Richard, *ti voglio bene.*"

I had just started learning Italian so I didn't understand her. "What?"

"Ti voglio bene," she repeated more slowly.

"You want what?" I asked.

She rolled her eyes, then exclaimed in English, "I love you!"

Ti voglio bene in Italian means literally "I want good for you," or "I wish you well." This is precisely the kind of love I'm proposing.

This definition of love is not how most vehicles of pop culture portray love—what psychologists call "limerence," a psychological state of deep infatuation that doesn't last. The form of love I'm describing is something much surer and better. It is something much holier. It is not as much about desiring a person as it is to desire their well-being, their physical, mental, and spiritual growth.

Metaphorically, this form of love is not the beautiful, briefly blooming rosebud, but its thorny stem—the flower's protection and source of all nourishment and life.

This love is selfless in that it frees the ego from

narcissism and the constant clamoring of me, me, me.

Sadly, for some, this type of love might be hard to comprehend or even believe in, but it does exist. I've experienced it. I've seen it in my wife and children. I've seen it in my friends. I've seen it in my better self.

A little more than a decade ago, my then seven-year-old daughter, Abigail, demonstrated this kind of love at a public swimming pool.

Abigail had just learned how to swim but was still fearful of the deep water, so she stayed in the shallow end of the pool. At the same time, her three-year-old brother Michael, who couldn't swim, was wearing water wings, and floating in the deep end.

I was sitting on a lounge chair at the side of the pool reading a book when I heard Abi shouting. I looked over to see her in the deep end of the pool holding on to Michael's arm, struggling to keep her head above water.

"Abi!" I shouted. "Let go of him!"

The two continued to struggle.

"Abi!" I shouted again. "You're going to drown both of you! Let go of him right now!"

Then the lifeguard did what I should have done, he dove into the pool and pulled the two children out of the water. Only after they were on dry ground did I learn what had happened.

Michael had jumped into the pool with his arms extended above his head. One of his water wings came completely off and the other had slid up to his elbow, leaving him partially submerged. In spite of her great fear of deep water, Abigail had jumped in to save her brother. Her selfless love was stronger than her fear.

I also saw this kind of love demonstrated by a stranger on an airplane flight to St. Louis. I had just taken my seat in the first-class section of the plane when a young woman walked past me carrying a child in her arms. I noticed that the woman was crying.

As we prepared to take off, the young man seated across the aisle from me suddenly stood up and walked to the back of the plane. Then, a moment later the young woman with the child walked up and sat down in the seat he'd left vacant. The young man had given this woman his first-class seat.

The woman was still crying and struggling with her toddler, so after takeoff I gave her little girl my iPad to play with and asked how I could help. The woman said to me, "I'm sorry I'm such a mess. My husband died last night. My little girl is too young to understand, she keeps asking for her daddy."

Having spent many years interacting with those who have lost loved ones, I spent the next hour consoling the woman and helping her make plans for her new life. After the flight, I stopped the young man who had given up his seat and asked him if he knew that the woman had just lost her husband.

"No," he said. "She just looked like she needed some help."

Both my daughter and this young man demonstrated the beauty and power of this selfless form of love.*

THE WORK OF LOVE

What the fourth door proposes is an act of will: an intellectual and spiritual decision to re-create our mental maps on the basis of love. And, as I've described, this holy love is not a hole to fall into, it's a plant to be cultivated, nourished and, ultimately, harvested. It is work.

We don't often think of love as work, but that's precisely what real love is. If it seems that I am attempting to remove mysticism from love, that's exactly what I am trying to do (a bold move for a romance writer). But what is lost in mysticism is more than made up for in honesty, longevity, and vitality.

---

* The young man's name is Ali W. Palmer. He's the founder of a company called LifeCon and is a life coach.

Noted psychologist and sociologist Erich Fromm taught that love is not only an act of will but a skill to be developed—a proven psychological truth.

It is a truth I've proven myself. As a teenager, I became enamored of the works of Og Mandino. In his most famous book, *The Greatest Salesman in the World,* he wrote a daily affirmation that began:

> *I will greet this day with love in my heart. For this is the greatest secret of success in all ventures.*

Following Mandino's counsel, I read his four-page affirmation three times a day for thirty days and followed the affirmation's instructions to greet everyone I met with love, by looking into their eyes and saying to myself, *I love you.* I was amazed at the potency of this little exercise and how quickly my perception of the world changed, how fear vanished and how strangers became friends.

PROJECTING LOVE

Og Mandino's affirmation reminds me of the Indian salutation *Namaste*. As commonly used, *Namaste* is a respectful greeting derived from Sanskrit, which means, literally, *I bow to you*. But the word has a much deeper spiritual significance than obeisance. *Namaste,* and it's older variant, *Namaskar,* implies the belief that divinity is in all of us. In acknowledging this oneness, we honor the god or divine spark in the person we are greeting. I like this. Imagine if we greeted everyone we met as a portion of God. The result would be powerful indeed.

I once heard one of the world's religious leaders say to a small audience I was seated in, "I appreciate the abundance of love and kindness you have shown me this evening. I can only imagine what kind of a world this would be if everyone was given the love you have given me."

How can we share this kind of universal love in our lives? Remember, Erich Fromm taught that love is a skill. There are techniques of love that we can master. One technique I have personally used (similar to Mandino's affirmation) is to project love on those around us whether we actually come in contact with them or not.

For instance, you're late for picking up the kids from school and annoyed because you're stuck in traffic due to a car accident. As you approach the accident scene, instead of projecting anger for the inconvenience they've caused you, say to yourself, *I'm sorry this happened to you. I hope you're okay and don't suffer any permanent harm from this accident.*

Just think of how much better you will feel with less stress and anger. Think of how much better you will view yourself.

Or, as a waitress approaches your table, you think, *Thank you for serving me. I hope you are having a good evening and all is well in your life.*

Even unspoken, these thoughts will shine in your eyes, resonate in your voice and fill your soul with love. Remember, since love is a skill, it will grow with use and practice.

And what if your love is not shared by the person you bestow it on? It makes absolutely no difference. The form of love we're talking about always lifts the giver more than the receiver. In fact, it protects the giver—buffers him and strengthens him from the less enlightened.

LOVE IN SERVICE

Service is love made visible.
—STEPHEN COLBERT

While, arguably, love may exist in a vacuum, it would never voluntarily stay there. Love *is* what love *does*. We do not send away our loved ones so we can learn how to love them. Love is hands-on, on-the-job training. We improve love through the work and practice of love. We develop love through service.

I wanted to teach my teenage daughter, Jenna, this lesson, so I took her on a daddy-daughter date to the Amazon jungles of Peru on a humanitarian mission. It turned into an extraordinary adventure. We canoed over caiman-infested waters, hiked deep into the jungle with machetes, and on one of our excursions we ran out of food so we had to eat piranha. (Piranha is easy to catch. It tastes like chicken.)

In the city of Puerto Maldonado, we set up a medical clinic, and for three days we served the impoverished Quechuan natives, checking their eyesight and handing out free eyeglasses.

A week later, on our way back home, I asked Jenna what she had learned from the experience. She replied, "I'll get back to you, Dad."

Twelve hours later, we were in Chicago's O'Hare airport waiting for our final connection home when I noticed that Jenna was crying. I asked her what was wrong. She replied, "We have so much and they have so little. It's not fair."

"No," I said, "it's not."

She was quiet for a moment, then said, "I

know what I learned. We love those whom we serve."

I remember thinking, *That's right, honey. That's why we went to the jungle.* I wonder if every time one of us figures this out, God is likewise thinking, *That's right, my beloved. That's why I sent you to the jungle.*

The first of the Four Doors is to believe there's a reason you were born. The fourth door is the greatest of reasons you were born: to learn how to love—to love God and to love others. They are the same thing, really. We cannot love God without loving His children.

We didn't come to this earth to make a name for ourselves just so time could erase it. We didn't come here to compile material possessions just so they could be parceled off and quibbled over at our deaths. We came to learn how to love.

In creating our love-centered maps, we must recognize that love is more than our destination— it's the back roads and byways, the high-speed expressway and the peaks and valleys. It's everything. There are no detours. There are no shortcuts. Love is the destination and the journey. Love is the way.

> . . . Love, for the sake of love, will always be enough. And if our lives are but a single flash in the dark hollow of eternity, then, if, but for the briefest of moments, we shine—then how brilliantly our light has burned. And as the starlight knows no boundary of space or time, so, too, our illumination will shine forth throughout all eternity, for darkness has no power to quell such light. And this is a lesson we must all learn and take to heart—that all light is eternal and all love is light. And it must forever be so.
>
> —From my book *The Letter*

If you choose to adopt just one of the doors, make it this one. Indeed, the fourth door leads to all the others. With a love-centered map, we intuitively feel our divine worth and the importance of our mission on earth, we instinctively seek freedom, and we, motivated by love, will magnify our lives.

Conclusion

Learning to live the Four Doors is like learning to play chess: an hour to learn the rules, a lifetime to master them. Is it worth the effort? Yes! A resounding yes!

Truthfully, what other reasonable choice is there? Would you want to live a purposeless life, enslaved in your own mind? Would you knowingly choose to live small and without love? If you think about it, there is no happy alternative to the Four

Doors. Still, you have the choice. And, as I wrote in the beginning of this book, *The Four Doors* is all about choice. You have the choice, beginning right now, to live a more abundant life, a life of joy, freedom, and meaning. I encourage you to walk through the Four Doors. Even if this were to be your last day on earth, it is still a choice worth making and a journey worth taking. Again, I wish you well on your journey.

About the Author

Richard Paul Evans is the author of twenty-four consecutive *New York Times* bestselling novels. He has won the American Mothers Book Award, *Romantic Times* Best Women's Novel of the Year Award, two first-place Storytelling World Awards for his children's books, the German Lesepreis Gold Award, and three Wilbur Awards from the Religion Communicators Council. His books have been translated into more than eighteen languages, and more than seventeen million copies of his books are in print worldwide. He has appeared on *The Today Show, Glenn Beck,* CNN, C-SPAN, CNBC, and *Entertainment Tonight,* and has been written about in *Time, Newsweek,* the *New York Times,* the *Washington Post,* the *Wall Street Journal*, *Family Circle*, *People* magazine, *USA Today,* and *Good Housekeeping,* as well as hundreds of newspapers across America and Europe. Evans was featured on the first *Reader's Digest* cover of this century.

At the age of thirty, Evans was the recipient of the Ernst & Young Entrepreneur of the Year Lifetime Achievement Award. He is also the founder of The Christmas Box House International, an organization dedicated to helping abused and neglected children. More than fifty thousand children have been served by Evans's foundation. He is the recipient of the *Washington Times* Humanitarian of the Century Award and the Volunteers of America National Empathy Award. He lives in Salt Lake City, Utah, with his wife, Keri, and their five children.

Join The Four Doors Community

Speaking

To book Richard for a speaking event email your request to: info@richardpaulevans.com

Facebook

Join *The Four Doors Society* Facebook page for daily inspirational messages from Richard Paul Evans and interaction with others who value the Four Door principles.

Mailing List

Join author Richard Paul Evans's mailing list by going to www.richardpaulevans.com